HORROR

M·O·V·I·E·S

HORROR
M·O·V·I·E·S

by Tom Powers

Lerner Publications Company
Minneapolis

Acknowledgments

The photographs in this book are reproduced through the courtesy of: pp. 1, 2, 11, 13, 17, 19, 30, 32, 33, 34, 37, 39, 40, 43, 44, 45, 47, 49, 50, 53, 55, Wisconsin Center for Film and Theater Research; pp. 3, 62, 66, 67, 70, 72, 75, 78, Hollywood Book and Poster Co.; pp. 8, 18, 21, 25, 29, Museum of Modern Art/Film Stills Archive; pp. 26, 31, 57, 59, 64, 77, Photofest.

Front and back cover photographs courtesy of Wisconsin Center for Film and Theater Research.

LIBRARY OF CONGRESS CATALOGING-IN-PUBLICATION DATA

Powers, Tom (Tom J.)
  Horror movies / by Tom Powers.
    p. cm.
  Bibliography: p.
  Includes index.
  Summary: Describes the characteristics and appeal of horror movies and discusses the plot and the making of some of the more famous of the genre.
  ISBN 0-8225-1636-5 (lib. bdg.)
  1. Horror films—History and criticism—Juvenile literature.
2. Horror films—Production and direction—Juvenile literature.
3. Horror films—History and criticism. 4. Horror films—Production and direction. [1. Horror films.] I. Title
PN1995.9.H6P65 1989
791.43'09'0916—dc19   88-35983
                                                    CIP
                                                    AC

Manufactured in the United States of America

1 2 3 4 5 6 7 8 9 10 99 98 97 96 95 94 93 92 91 90 89

Contents

Introduction

At the heart of the horror movie lies a fear of the unknown. What happens to us when we die? What makes some people evil? Are there magic powers in the world that science cannot explain? And most of all, is there evil hidden within our own souls?

In monster movies, beasts come from faraway places. They come from exotic lands, from outer space, or from under the sea. In horror movies, on the other hand, the beasts come from within people. Horror movies are about people with sick minds. Sometimes these people have brought the sickness on themselves; other times they are simply innocent victims.

Often the evil person in a horror movie has done something very wrong, something that has driven him or her insane. The crazy young motel-keeper in *Psycho* has murdered his mother. The mad preacher in *The Night of the Hunter* is a murderer of women. Freddy Kruger in *A*

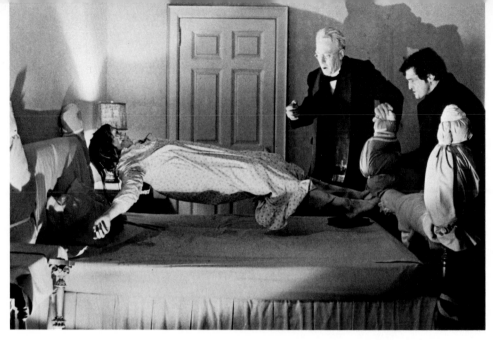

In horror movies, even innocent people can become victims, such as the 12-year-old girl who is possessed by the devil in *The Exorcist.*

Nightmare on Elm Street is a child-killer. All these men were driven insane by the wickedness of their deeds.

Other figures in horror movies, however, are tormented by powers beyond their control. Twelve-year-old Regan in *The Exorcist* is possessed by the devil. The zombie-woman Jessica in *I Walked with a Zombie* is the victim of a curse. These characters are not responsible for what happened to them; strange and horrible forces have taken over their minds.

Horror movies seem to tell us that no one is safe. Even if you lead a good life, the devil might get you or Freddy Kruger might chase you in your dreams. And if you give in to wickedness, you will become a kind of human monster—a person without a soul.

The figure of the vampire combines both these ideas of evil and innocence. For this reason, the vampire is one of the most popular figures in horror movies.

The vampire is an evil character; he murders people and sucks their blood. Yet at the same time, the vampire is a victim. He cannot help being the way he is. The vampire is like a person who wishes he could take back his wicked deed. He is like a killer who wishes he had never pulled the trigger, but it is too late. Just as the killer is sentenced to die, the vampire is condemned to a living death. He prowls the earth at night, never to see the sunshine.

Since the vampire cannot die, he cannot know the happiness of heaven. The object the vampire hates most is the crucifix—the Christian symbol of humanity's salvation and hope for eternal happiness. When Count Dracula covers his eyes at the sight of a crucifix, he gives audiences hope that their fate will be happier than his.

Many horror movies appeal to audiences' belief in life after death. It is not surprising, then, that scientists and doctors are often made to look foolish in horror movies. Science has never been able to answer the question, "Is there life after death?"

In *The Exorcist*, when Regan is possessed by the devil, her doctors claim that the problem is merely a disease. In *A Nightmare on Elm Street*, Nancy Thompson's doctor says that Freddy Kruger is just a bad dream—even though this "bad dream" is killing all the teenagers in the neighborhood. Dr. Maxwell in *I Walked with a Zombie* refuses to recognize that his patient, Jessica, is one of the "undead." Over and over again, horror movies repeat the message that there are mysteries that science cannot explain—and the greatest mystery is death.

Death comes to everyone, yet the victims in many horror movies are children or young women. In part, this is because women and children are the most vulnerable members of our society. They are most likely to be beaten up or hurt or mistreated.

Children are important in horror movies for another reason. Almost everyone was once badly frightened as a child—too frightened to run, too frightened even to scream. Most adults forget what that kind of fear is like. Adults learn how to deal with scary situations or avoid them. But almost every adult carries inside him or her a buried memory of being really scared.

Sometimes that buried memory influences the way people behave. People may be afraid of flying, of dogs, of working at certain jobs, or even of making new friends—all because of something that happened long ago, something they may not even remember. That is part of the reason why horror movies are so popular. Horror movies bring old fears to the surface. But horror movies allow people to be scared in a safe way, in a movie theater, surrounded by hundreds of other people who are also scared.

And although they may be frightening, horror movies can make the idea of death itself a little less frightening. For as Count Dracula says, "There are far worse things awaiting man than death."

Note: The following abbreviations are used in this book:
  b/w black and white
  dir director
  pro producer
  st starring
  sp eff special effects

DRACULA

(1931)

b/w
dir Tod Browning
pro Carl Laemmle, Jr.
st Bela Lugosi, Edward Van Sloan,
    Dwight Frye, Helen Chandler,
    David Manners

A vampire is a person who has died and yet still walks the earth. Vampires attack people at night and drink their blood. If you are bitten by a vampire, you could die, or you might turn into a vampire yourself.

Many countries have myths about vampires. In Scotland, people once believed that if a cat jumped over a corpse, the dead person would become a vampire. Chinese vampires traditionally are green and glow in the dark. Russian vampires suck blood from their victim's heart. European vampires go for the neck.

By some estimates, nearly 600 vampire movies have been made. The most famous is the 1931 film called *Dracula*, one of the first great American horror films.

"To Die, to Be Really Dead—That Must Be Glorious"

A horse-drawn coach rushes down a steep, narrow road in the mountainous country of Transylvania. When the coach finally comes to a halt, it is nearly sunset. Most of the passengers climb down into the dusty courtyard of an old inn. But one passenger, a young Englishman named Renfield, announces that he plans to go on to the Borgo Pass that night. "Count Dracula's carriage will be waiting there for me," he says.

At the mention of Count Dracula, the local people fall silent. The innkeeper asks Renfield not to travel farther that night, explaining that there are vampires at the castle. "Dracula and his wives—they take the form of wolves and bats. They leave their coffins at night and feed on the blood of the living."

Renfield smiles politely at the superstitious innkeeper and starts to climb back into the coach. The innkeeper's wife rushes over and places a crucifix around Renfield's neck. "Wear this," she tells Renfield, "for your mother's sake. It will protect you." Renfield tucks the small cross into his vest pocket.

Near midnight, Renfield's coach reaches the Borgo Pass. The terrified coach driver stops just long enough for Renfield to climb down. Then the driver throws Renfield's luggage on the ground and hurries away.

A small carriage is waiting for Renfield. Sitting atop it, wrapped in a black cape, is a tall, silent figure with strange, hypnotic eyes. He gestures for Renfield to get in.

On the way to Count Dracula's castle, Renfield leans out the window to speak to the driver. He is startled to see that the driver has disappeared. A large gray bat seems to be guiding the carriage instead.

When Renfield enters Count Dracula's castle, he finds

a huge, deserted chamber. Rats and armadillos scurry across the dirt-covered stone floor. Giant spiderwebs hang from the ceiling. Renfield is amazed by the strange place. He is even more amazed when he turns around and finds a tall, elegant man standing in front of him. "I am Dracula," the man says.

The Count leads Renfield up the castle's great stone staircase. Outside, wolves can be heard howling in the distance. Noticing that the sound frightens Renfield, Dracula smiles sweetly. "Listen to them," he says. "Children of the night. What music they make."

The Count has prepared a meal for Renfield, and he pours him a glass of wine.

Count Dracula eyes a cut on Renfield's finger.

"Aren't you drinking?" Renfield asks.

"I never drink...wine," the Count replies.

Over dinner, Renfield tells Dracula that he has arranged for the Count to lease Carfax Abbey in England. He assures the Count that no one in England knows he is coming.

As Renfield puts the lease papers in his briefcase, he cuts his finger on a paper clip. Blood spurts from the cut, and Dracula, seeing it, moves closer to Renfield. An odd, hungry look comes over the Count's face. Before the Count can grab Renfield's bleeding finger, however, the small crucifix tumbles out of Renfield's vest pocket. The sight of the crucifix sends Dracula reeling backwards, throwing his arm over his eyes.

Later that night, as Renfield prepares for bed, he feels dizzy. Too late, he realizes that Dracula put sleeping powder in his wine. Renfield collapses on the floor. Count Dracula enters the room, stoops low over the fallen young man, and bites into his neck.

A few days later, Dracula and Renfield are on board a sailing ship, bound for England. Deep in the hold, Renfield opens Dracula's coffin. "The sun is gone," Renfield says in a mad whisper. As Dracula rises from his dirt-filled coffin, Renfield shrinks back like a fearful dog. His hair is mussed and he has a wild look in his eyes. He has become Count Dracula's slave.

When the ship finally drifts into an English harbor, the police find the entire crew dead. Only one passenger seems to have survived, a madman who sucks the blood out of ants and flies. The police take this madman—Renfield—to a special hospital run by Dr. Seward. The hospital is located next door to Carfax Abbey.

Before long, a number of murder victims are found at

night on the streets of London. The victims are brought to Dr. Seward's hospital for examination. Seward makes an unusual discovery. On the throat of each victim are two small holes.

One night Dr. Seward attends the opera with his daughter Mina and two of her friends. At the theater, an elegantly dressed gentleman introduces himself as their new neighbor. His name, he says, is Count Dracula.

Mina's friend Lucy Weston is fascinated by the Count. He is rich and mysterious and lives in a huge, gloomy abbey. To Lucy, Count Dracula seems like a man who understands the deepest mysteries of life and death. "To die," the Count tells Lucy, "to be really dead—that must be glorious. There are far worse things awaiting man than death."

Later that night, after Lucy has gone to bed, a large bat flies in her bedroom window. In an instant, Count Dracula is leaning over Lucy, sucking the blood from her neck. Lucy does not die, but becomes, like Dracula, a vampire.

At Dr. Seward's hospital, a scientist named Van Helsing asks to see Renfield. He tests a sample of Renfield's blood and pronounces Renfield "undead—a vampire." Dr. Seward tells Van Helsing that he does not believe in vampires.

That night, as Mina sleeps, Dracula visits her room and sucks her blood. The delicate young woman does not die, but her personality starts to change. She seems tired and lifeless. She tells her fiance, John Harker, that she has been having terrible dreams.

Van Helsing overhears Mina talking to John. He asks to look at Mina's throat. There he finds two little bite marks. "What could have caused them, Professor?" John asks. Just then, a maid introduces a visitor—Count Dracula.

Dracula has never met Van Helsing before, but he says

he has heard of the scientist. As Dracula turns to talk to Mina and John, Van Helsing opens a small silver box that has a mirror inside its lid. Van Helsing can see John and Mina reflected in the mirror, but Dracula, standing between them, is invisible. Vampires, Van Helsing knows, show no reflection in a mirror.

Van Helsing tells Dracula he wants to show him something. The Count politely looks into the box. When he sees the mirror, he slaps the box out of Van Helsing's hands. "For one who has not lived even a single lifetime," Dracula says, "you are a wise man, Van Helsing."

When Dracula has gone, Van Helsing explains to Dr. Seward that "a vampire is a being that lives after its death by drinking the blood of the living. Its power lasts only from sunset to sunrise. During the hours of the day, it must rest in the earth in which it was buried." Van Helsing says that Dracula must have brought boxes of earth with him to England from Transylvania.

Meanwhile, Mina has left the house. Dracula lifts his cape and wraps it around her. A few minutes later, a maid rushes into the house, screaming that Mina's body is lying on the lawn.

Mina is alive, but she knows that Dracula is beginning to control her. Mina tells her fiance that he must not see her again. As she speaks, she looks at John's neck as if she wants to sink her teeth into it. Just then, a bat flies into the room. John chases the bat away. Mina, however, seems to be talking to it. "Yes," she says, "yes, I will."

Van Helsing tells John that they must find Dracula's coffin and kill him by driving a wooden stake through his heart. That night, Dracula confronts Van Helsing in the Sewards' living room. Dracula fixes Van Helsing with his powerful stare and signals for the old man to come closer,

Dracula can't resist the allure of Mina's neck.

but Van Helsing resists. Dracula leaps at the scientist, but Van Helsing pulls a crucifix out of his coat pocket. Dracula runs out of the house.

The vampire has not given up, however. He returns to Mina's bedroom and carries her away. Meanwhile, John and Van Helsing see Renfield and follow him to Carfax Abbey. Peering into the Abbey through barred windows, John sees Dracula and Mina. Dracula is leading Mina down a long flight of stairs. He finds Renfield blocking his path. "Don't kill me," the madman sobs. Dracula throws Renfield down the stairs, and he tumbles to his death.

John and Van Helsing find an entrance to the Abbey. They chase Dracula through its huge, dirty rooms, but the vampire disappears just as the sun comes up. Pushing open a large, creaking door, Van Helsing discovers a room with three coffins. Raising the lid of the first coffin, he finds Count Dracula. Van Helsing breaks the lid of the coffin and makes a sharp, pointed stake. He places the stake above the vampire's heart, then pounds it into him.

Dracula's Carfax Abbey is a huge, scary place.

Van Helsing opens the other coffins, fearing that he will find Mina inside one of them. They are empty. Suddenly, Mina calls to John from a far corner of the room. John rushes to her and hugs her. "We thought he'd killed you, dear," he says.

Mina, released from the vampire's power, holds John close to her. "The daylight stopped him," she says. As Van Helsing looks down upon the dead vampire, Mina and John walk up the Abbey stairs and out into the sunlight. In the distance, church bells are ringing.

THE MAKING AND UNMAKING OF A STAR

When sound movies first began to be made in the late 1920s, many silent-film actors found themselves out of work. These actors were not trained to speak lines of dialogue, and often their voices did not fit the characters they were asked to play. Foreign-born actors in particular had trouble finding jobs because of their thick accents.

Actor Bela Lugosi lounges in his studio.

For the Hungarian-born actor Bela Lugosi, however, the "talkies" provided a wonderful opportunity. Lugosi had been performing in the United States in a stage version of *Dracula*, so he was used to dialogue. His deep voice had just enough of an accent to make him sound "foreign" and "mysterious." When Lugosi first announced, "I am Drac...u...la," movie audiences across America were thrilled and frightened. *Dracula* became Universal Studios' biggest hit of 1931.

For his next movie, Lugosi was asked to play the part of a monster brought to life by a mad scientist. Lugosi turned down the part when he learned that his face would be hidden beneath a thick layer of makeup. The part of Frankenstein's monster went instead to Boris Karloff.

Boris Karloff went on to become a great star in horror movies, playing many different roles. Bela Lugosi, on the other hand, rarely found roles as well suited for him as Dracula was. Although he acted in movies for more than 20 years, Lugosi's fans always identified him with the charming, wicked vampire. When Lugosi died in 1956, he was buried, at his request, wearing the black cape of Count Dracula.

I WALKED WITH A ZOMBIE

b/w
dir Jacques Tourneur
pro Val Lewton
st Frances Dee, Tom Conway,
    James Ellison, Christine Gordon

Producer Val Lewton's wife once said, "I would never go to see a movie called *I Walked with a Zombie* unless somebody dragged me there." Movie audiences in 1943 apparently agreed with her, and few people bothered to see the film. If they had, they would have seen a well-crafted, disturbing motion picture.

The bosses at Val Lewton's studio, RKO, did not give him much money to spend on his films, and they did not let him choose his films' titles. What the studio bosses did do was let Lewton make his movies the way he wanted. In horror films like *Cat People, The Body Snatcher,* and *I Walked with a Zombie*, Lewton proved that there is more to horror than bloodshed and violence. He showed how horror can be created through music, lighting, editing, and realistic characters in believable situations.

"Jessica Is Not Insane. She Is Dead."

Betsy Connell, a young Canadian nurse, sails to the West Indies to begin an exciting new job as a nurse for the sick wife of a wealthy factory owner.

In the West Indies, Betsy is met by Paul Holland, her new employer. Together they sail on Paul's boat to the small island of St. Sebastian. From the deck of the boat, Betsy watches the sun sink into the ocean. She is thrilled by the beauty of the islands. Paul Holland, however, seems to read Betsy's thoughts. He says, "There is no beauty here, only death and decay."

Betsy likes Paul right away, but she feels that a powerful sadness is buried inside him. Paul is always polite, yet sometimes his words are cruel.

When Paul's boat lands at St. Sebastian, a horse and buggy is waiting to take Betsy to the Holland estate. Inside the walls of the estate, Betsy finds a beautiful courtyard lined with tropical flowers. In the center of the courtyard is a fountain built around a ship's wooden figurehead, a statue of the martyr Saint Sebastian. The saint's body is pierced by iron arrows. As the water from the fountain flows past the arrows, the figurehead seems to be bleeding.

That night at dinner, Betsy meets Paul Holland's half-brother, Wesley Rand. Wes is very different from Paul. Unlike Paul, who went to British schools and speaks with a British accent, Wes was educated in the U.S. While Paul seems stiff and formal, Wes is joking and friendly.

At dinner, Betsy is startled by the sound of drums beating in the distance. Wes makes fun of her. "The jungle drums," he says in a spooky voice. "Mysterious, eerie."

Actually, Wes explains, the drums are a kind of factory whistle, calling the workers to the Hollands' sugar factory.

Before she goes to bed that night, Betsy stands by her window, looking into the courtyard. A tall woman dressed in a flowing white gown drifts across the courtyard. The woman's eyes look empty, as if there is no life behind them. She disappears through a door that leads into a tower at the edge of the garden.

Betsy tries to sleep, but the sound of crying wakes her. She puts on her robe, crosses the courtyard, and opens the tower door. Inside the tower, Betsy walks up a long flight of stone steps. At the top of the steps she sees the woman in the white gown. The woman moves toward Betsy like a ghost. Frightened, Betsy backs away, but the woman keeps coming after her.

Just as Betsy screams for help, Paul Holland enters the tower. He calls his servants to take the woman in white back to her bedroom. The woman, Paul explains to Betsy, is his wife, Jessica.

The next morning, Betsy joins the local doctor in Jessica's bedroom. "She makes a beautiful zombie, doesn't she?" Dr. Maxwell jokes. He tells Betsy that the people of St. Sebastian believe Jessica's condition is the result of a curse that turned her into a walking dead woman, a zombie. In fact, the doctor says, Jessica fell ill with a tropical fever that damaged her spine. "The result is what you see, a woman without any willpower. A sleepwalker who will never be awakened."

A few days later, Betsy decides to explore the town of St. Sebastian. There she bumps into Wes Rand, who takes her to a sunny outdoor cafe. As they talk, Betsy realizes that Wes is very bitter towards his half-brother Paul. Wes says that Paul made Jessica's life miserable.

"He uses words like other men use their fists," Wes says.

In another part of the cafe, a local band plays calypso songs, story-songs popular in the Caribbean Islands. One of the songs tells the story of two brothers who loved the same woman. The woman had planned to leave her husband and run away with his brother. But on the very night they were going to run away, the woman fell sick. She never recovered, the singer says, and now there is "shame and sorrow on the family."

When he hears this song, Wes grows very angry. Betsy understands that the song is about Wes and Jessica and Paul. The two brothers are in love with the same woman. To make things worse, Betsy herself is falling in love with Paul. She decides to show her love through a selfless act. She will nurse Jessica back to health, so that Paul can be happy again with his wife.

Betsy asks Dr. Maxwell to perform a dangerous treatment that will shock Jessica out of her sleepwalking condition. The treatment might cure Jessica, or it might kill her.

As Paul waits for news of the treatment's success, Wes arrives and begins yelling at his half-brother. He accuses Paul of not loving Jessica, of secretly hoping that she will die. When Betsy steps out of Jessica's room, the two brothers turn to her hopefully. The attempted cure has failed, Betsy says. "She's alive, that's all."

The next day, Paul's servant Alma tells Betsy about the voodoo rituals practiced by the natives of St. Sebastian. Voodoo is a kind of witchcraft. In voodoo, objects like dolls or animal bones are believed to have magical powers. These powers can be used to cast spells over people.

Betsy does not believe in voodoo, but she is impressed by what Alma tells her. In town, Betsy stops by the local

As Betsy leads the zombie Jessica to the Houmfort, they encounter frightening objects, like a dead sheep hanging from a tree.

infirmary, where Mrs. Rand, Paul and Wesley's mother, gives out medicine to the islanders. Betsy asks Mrs. Rand if a voodoo ceremony might help Jessica. "It might be dangerous," Mrs. Rand warns.

That night, as a hot wind blows across the island, Betsy takes Jessica to the "Houmfort," the place where the islanders gather to perform voodoo rituals. Betsy leads Jessica by the hand, guiding her through fields of sugar cane that towers over their heads. The path to the

25

A zombie-like man guards the entrance to the Houmfort.

Houmfort is marked by frightening objects: a horse's skull on a stick and a dead sheep hanging from a tree.

At a bend in the path, Betsy nearly bumps into a tall, fierce-looking man. Like Jessica's, the man's eyes look empty. Betsy leads Jessica past this ghostly guard, who seems not to notice them. When they have passed, the guard follows them.

At the Houmfort, the people of the island sing and dance with wild jumps and shouts. One dancer, who waves a saber in the air, seems to cast a spell over a woman dancer. She slowly collapses to the ground.

Beyond the dancers, people stand in line outside a small wooden booth, waiting to talk to the voodoo priest. Betsy leads Jessica to the booth and whispers to the priest that she has come for help. A door in the booth opens, and a pair of hands grabs Betsy and pulls her inside. Jessica is left standing alone outside as the islanders circle around her.

Inside the booth, Betsy is startled to discover Mrs. Rand standing next to the voodoo priest. The old woman tells Betsy to take Jessica home. She says that voodoo rituals are nothing more than superstition. Disappointed, Betsy steps outside the booth and begins to lead Jessica away. But the islanders do not want them to leave. Betsy has to push her way past several people. She rushes Jessica through the cane fields, frequently looking back to make sure that no one is chasing them.

The next morning, the jungle drums are pounding. The people of St. Sebastian believe they have seen a zombie. They will not rest until Jessica is sent back to them—or until she is destroyed.

Paul tells Betsy that he wants her to return to Canada. He does not want her hurt by the growing scandal that surrounds his family. Paul believes that he himself, through his cruel words, drove Jessica insane.

Paul's mother is upset when she hears him talking to Betsy this way. Mrs. Rand has a secret that she can hold inside no longer. "Jessica is not insane," she says. "She is dead. I did it."

Mrs. Rand tells Paul how she long ago entered into the islanders' voodoo ceremonies. At first she did it merely to help the people. However, when she learned that Jessica was going to leave Paul and run away with Wesley, a terrible fear gripped Mrs. Rand. She saw her family being destroyed by scandal. So Mrs. Rand called on the voodoo gods to turn Jessica into a zombie. That very night, the life went out of Jessica.

Paul and Betsy are sure that Mrs. Rand is mistaken. Jessica is ill, but she is not a zombie. Wes thinks his mother is right, though. That night he asks Betsy to give Jessica enough medicine to kill her. When Betsy refuses, Wes begins to sob. "I can't make you believe that she's already dead," he says.

The evening air is hot and still as a crowd of people gathers at the Houmfort. The nightly voodoo ritual begins. Someone has made a doll that looks like Jessica. The "saber-man" dances over the doll, then begins to wave his hands, gesturing for the doll to come to him. The doll rises off the ground and moves toward the saber-man, as if he is pulling it by an invisible string.

At the same moment, Jessica rises from her bed and walks into the courtyard of the Holland estate. Her path is blocked by a locked gate. As Jessica stands at the gate, Wes watches her from the patio. He loves her and cannot stand to see her condemned to a living death any longer. He opens the gate and lets Jessica out, then reaches across

As part of the voodoo ritual, the saber-man directs the doll, which represents Jessica, toward him.

to the figurehead of Saint Sebastian. He pulls a long, sharp arrow out of the wooden figure. Holding the arrow in his hand like a sword, Wes hurries after Jessica.

At the Houmfort, the voodoo doll has magically moved across the ground into the hands of the saber-man. Taking a sharp needle, the saber-man stabs the doll. Just at that moment, Wes Rand stabs his arrow into Jessica's chest, setting her free at last from her living death.

Wes picks up Jessica's lifeless body and carries it to the ocean. Silently, sadly, he walks into the water. The ocean waves break over the unhappy lovers.

Later that night, a group of islanders go fishing with torches and spears. Instead of fish, they find a body floating in the sea. Forming a silent procession, the people of St. Sebastian carry Jessica home. As Betsy watches the islanders enter the courtyard, she remembers what Paul told her when she first arrived: "There is no beauty here, only death and decay."

"SOCK-IT-TO-THEM WAS BEING SACRIFICED FOR 'ARTY STUFF'"

Producer Val Lewton was not able to spend a lot of money on his films, but he did try to make them look and sound authentic. For *I Walked with a Zombie*, Lewton

Although *I Walked with a Zombie* was a subtle film, there was nothing subtle about the way it was advertised.

Val Lewton produced several low-budget horror films, including *Cat People* and *Isle of the Dead*. His work influenced the horror movie genre for years.

read every book on voodoo that he could find. He hired a calypso singer, Sir Lancelot, to perform the music in the cafe.

Lewton gave his crew precise instructions about what furniture should be placed in Jessica's room, what map should hang in Paul's study, and what lines the characters should speak. In one scene, for instance, Betsy is awakened by Paul's servant Alma squeezing her toe. "I didn't want to frighten you out of your sleep, miss," Alma says. "That's why I touched you farthest from your heart."

At first Lewton was not happy about making a film about zombies. Then he had an idea. He would base the film on the famous novel *Jane Eyre*, which tells the story of a young woman who leaves home to work for a strange man whose wife has an incurable illness. From this starting point, Lewton fashioned a story in which real characters with real feelings were exposed to the horrors of the unknown. For the most part, the studio bosses left Lewton alone, but they occasionally worried about *I Walked with a Zombie*. As one of the film's writers remembers, the bosses complained that "sock-it-to-them was being sacrificed for 'arty stuff'."

In *The Night of the Hunter*, Robert Mitchum plays a crazy preacher.
Notice the tattoos on his fingers.

THE NIGHT OF THE HUNTER

b/w
dir Charles Laughton
pro Paul Gregory
st Robert Mitchum, Shelley
　　Winters, Peter Graves, Billy
　　Chapin, Sally Jane Bruce,
　　Lillian Gish

The *Night of the Hunter* was the only film directed by Charles Laughton. Laughton was a famous actor, a huge, flabby-faced man with a voice that could make a whisper sound like rolling thunder.

To play Mrs. Cooper in the film, Laughton chose Lillian Gish, a great movie star from the era of silent films. Gish asked Laughton why he wanted her to play this important role. Laughton thought about it, then replied, "When I first went to the movies, people sat in their seats straight and leaned forward. Now they slump down, with their heads back or eat candy and popcorn. I want them to sit up straight again." Laughton knew that Lillian Gish had made moviegoers sit up and take notice for over 40 years.

Ben Harper asks his son John not to tell anyone where the stolen money is hidden. "I won't never tell about the money," John swears.

"Children Are Man at His Strongest"

John Harper is playing happily with his little sister Pearl when he sees a car speeding down the road. "It's Daddy," Pearl cries. She grabs her doll, Miss Jenny, and runs to meet him. John races past her.

John stops suddenly when he sees his father climb out of the car. Ben Harper is holding a gun in one hand and a wad of money in the other. He is bleeding from a bullet wound in his shoulder.

Police sirens wail in the distance as Ben Harper searches for a place to hide his stolen money, almost $10,000. He picks a place no one will guess. Ben tells John and Pearl that he stole the money for them. From now on, they must protect each other, he says, and they must never tell anyone where the money is hidden.

Two police cars roar into the yard. A half dozen policemen cautiously take Ben's gun away, then knock him to the ground and handcuff him. Young John Harper clutches his stomach in pain as he watches the police arrest his father.

Because he killed two guards while robbing the bank, Ben Harper is sentenced to die. During the last weeks of his life, Ben shares a prison cell with a man named Harry Powell. Powell claims to be a preacher, a man of God. In fact, he is an evil, insane man who has murdered a dozen women. Harry Powell thinks that God wants him to kill women. "There are things you do hate, Lord," Powell says in his strange prayers. "Perfume-smelling things, lacy things, things with curly hair."

The police do not know Powell is a murderer. He is serving a short sentence in prison for car theft, and he will soon be released. In the meantime, Powell tries to get Ben to tell him where the bank money is hidden. Ben refuses. Instead, he talks about the hard times that are sweeping the United States in the 1930s.

A few weeks later, on a moonlit night, John and Pearl are getting ready for bed. John tells Pearl a story about a rich king who was taken away by bad men. The king told his son to protect his gold while he was gone. "Before long," John says, "the bad men came back." Just then, a huge, black shadow fills the room. Pearl gasps in fear. Looking out the window, John sees a preacher, dressed all in black, standing by the streetlight in front of the house.

The next day, John visits Spoon's ice cream parlor, where his mother, Willa, works. When John looks in the window, he is shocked by what he sees. Pearl is sitting on the lap of a stranger—a preacher dressed all in black. John rushes inside to find out what is happening.

The preacher introduces himself as the Reverend Harry Powell. He says that he worked at the prison where John's father was hanged. John does not trust the man. He stares at the stranger's hands.

On the knuckles of Powell's left hand are tattooed the letters H-A-T-E. The letters L-O-V-E are tattooed on his right hand. "Would you like me to tell you the story of right hand-left hand?" the preacher asks.

Powell pretends that his hands are battling each other. He talks about life as a struggle between good and evil, love and hate. In the end, Powell's right hand forces his left hand down. Love is victorious. John's mother and Mr. and Mrs. Spoon are impressed by the preacher. But John just stares at Harry Powell, cool and suspicious.

A few nights later, John comes home after dark. The house is quiet. No one seems to be home. As John searches the house for his mother and sister, a black shadow falls over him. Harry Powell steps out of the darkness.

The preacher talks to John in a soft, kindly voice. He tells John that he is going to marry John's mother. John is terrified. "You ain't my dad, you'll never be my dad," he says. "You think you can make me tell, but I won't, I won't." As soon as he says these words, John slaps his hand over his mouth, but it is too late. Now Harry Powell knows that John knows where the money is hidden.

John's mother discovers too late Powell does not love her. Powell thinks that women are dirty. Hurt, confused, and disappointed, Willa falls more and more under Powell's spell. She even begins to mistrust her own son. When John tells her that Powell has been asking him about the money, Willa says, "John, you always make up that lie."

One night, however, Willa comes home late from work

Harry Powell pretends to be kind to the children, but John knows
better than to trust him.

and hears Powell talking to Pearl inside the house. The
preacher is asking the little girl where the money is hidden.
His voice becomes angrier and angrier. Finally he shouts
at Pearl, "You tell me, you little wretch, or I'll tear your
arm off." Willa rushes inside, not wanting to believe her
own ears. She smiles at Powell, waiting for him to explain.

The next day, Harry Powell visits Spoon's ice cream
parlor. He tells Mr. and Mrs. Spoon that Willa has run
away. "She'll not be back," he says. "I reckon I'm safe in
promising you that." He does not tell them that Willa is in
her car at the bottom of the river, with her throat slashed.

That night, Powell searches the house, looking for John
and Pearl. "Oh children," he cries in his soft, sweet voice.
"I can feel myself getting awful mad." When Powell finds
John and Pearl hiding in the cellar, he forces them to tell
him where the money is hidden. Hoping to get a chance
to escape, John says the money is buried beneath the
cellar floor.

Powell keeps the children nearby while he searches the cellar by candlelight. The floor, he discovers, is concrete. Throwing John over a barrel, Powell takes out his switch-blade knife, the same knife that he used to kill the children's mother. He prepares to cut John's throat. Sobbing, terrified, little Pearl cannot stand to see her brother in such danger. Finally she screams out their secret. "It's in my doll," she cries, "it's in my doll."

Harry Powell laughs out loud. The doll was the last place he would have thought to look. He sits down on the cellar floor, a happy smile on his face.

John seizes his opportunity. With one hand he snuffs out Powell's candle, throwing the cellar into darkness. With his other hand he knocks loose a board that sends a shelf full of preserves tumbling onto the preacher's head. John grabs Pearl, Pearl grabs her doll, and they run for the stairs. Furious, the preacher chases after them, his hands outstretched like Frankenstein's monster. John slams the cellar door on Powell's fingers.

John and Pearl run down to the river, where they find their father's old skiff. They climb into the small boat and John pushes it away from the shore. Just then, Powell comes crashing down the river bank, his knife held high. At the last moment, Powell slips in the mud, and the skiff slides just out of his reach. As the children float downriver, Harry Powell roars in anger like some monstrous animal.

Day after day, John and Pearl float down the Ohio River. One night they stop near a barn and climb into the hayloft to sleep. As the moon rises, John wakes to the sound of distant singing. Against the horizon, he sees Harry Powell riding a stolen horse, coming after the children. "Don't he never sleep?" John mutters to himself. He wakes Pearl and they hurry back to the boat.

One morning the exhausted, hungry children wake up to find that their boat has drifted ashore. A stern but kindly woman named Mrs. Cooper is towering over them. She takes the children back to her farm, which she runs as a home for lost children.

John and Pearl soon realize that the other children on the farm adore Mrs. Cooper. "I'm a strong tree," the gray-

Just in time, John and Pearl manage to escape the preacher by floating down the river in an old skiff.

Lillian Gish plays Mrs. Cooper, the kind old woman who befriends John, right, and Pearl, center.

haired lady likes to say, "with branches for many birds." John and Pearl quickly become part of Mrs. Cooper's big, makeshift family.

Before long, however, Harry Powell comes riding up to Mrs. Cooper's front gate. He says that he is looking for John and Pearl, his lost children, who have run away from Cincinnati, down the river. Powell's story makes Mrs. Cooper suspicious. She knows that John and Pearl's skiff must have floated downstream. They could not have paddled it against the river current from Cincinnati.

When Harry Powell tries to tell Mrs. Cooper his "right hand-left hand" story, she cuts him off. "He ain't my dad,"

John says to Mrs. Cooper. "No," says Mrs. Cooper, "and he ain't no preacher, neither."

Powell tries to snatch Pearl's doll, but John grabs it and dives under the front porch. The preacher pulls out his knife and crawls after the boy, but stops when he feels something tapping him on the back. He backs out from under the porch and looks up into the barrel of Mrs. Cooper's shotgun. Retreating to his horse, he yells, "You haven't heard the last of Harry Powell. I'll be back—when it's dark."

That night, Powell lurks outside the house, singing a hymn. Mrs. Cooper sits in a rocking chair, her shotgun held ready. She sings along with the phony preacher. Suddenly Powell vanishes. Mrs. Cooper gathers her children in the kitchen. She marches back and forth with her gun, telling Bible stories. A noise comes from the living room, and then Harry Powell pops up right in front of her. "I want them kids," Powell says. Mrs. Cooper blasts him.

Powell runs out of the house howling, apparently not badly hurt. The next morning, Mrs. Cooper phones the police. "I got something trapped in my barn," she says. The police come to arrest Harry Powell. As they throw him to the ground and start to handcuff him, a horrible memory rises up inside John of the last time he saw his father. John clutches his stomach in pain. Then he grabs Pearl's doll and rushes over to the policemen. He hits Harry with the doll over and over again. As he does so, the hidden money flies out. "I don't want it, I don't want it," John cries.

A trial follows, and Harry Powell is sentenced to be hanged for all the women he has killed.

That Christmas, John and Pearl finally discover what it means to be safe and happy. As the other children present gifts to Mrs. Cooper, John sneaks into the living room. He has no money to buy a present for Mrs. Cooper, so he wraps an apple in a lace doily and gives it to her. "That's the richest gift a body could have," Mrs. Cooper says. Her Christmas present to John is a new watch. "Children are man at his strongest," Mrs. Cooper tells John. "They abide."

"GET THAT CHILD AWAY FROM ME!"

The Night of the Hunter was designed to have the special feeling of a child's nightmare. The villain of the film, Harry Powell, is a kind of bogeyman, a scary, threatening figure who seems to pop up out of nowhere. No matter how far John and Pearl run, they cannot get away from him.

John and Pearl's trip down the river was actually filmed indoors at a movie studio in a large tank of water. By filming in the studio, the director and cameraman could control the scene. They added just the elements they wanted to give the scene a dreamlike quality: starry skies, chirping bullfrogs, hooting owls, and sparkling water.

The scene in which John sees Harry Powell riding up to the barn was also shot in the studio. For this scene, the director wanted the preacher to seem close yet far away at the same time. To accomplish this trick, he used a midget riding a tiny pony to substitute for the full-sized horse and actor. This trick made viewers think the smaller figures were farther away than they really were.

Director Charles Laughton enjoyed working with all the actors except the children. Laughton once overheard the film's star, Robert Mitchum, talking with Billy Chapin, the boy who played John. "Do you think John's frightened of the preacher?" Mitchum asked Billy.

"Nope," said Billy.

"Then you don't know the preacher," said Mitchum,

Charles Laughton was better
known as an actor than as a director.

"and you don't know John."

"Oh really?" said Billy in a smug way, defending his
acting talents. "That's probably why I just won the New
York Critics' Circle Prize."

"Get that child away from me!" roared Charles Laughton.

PSYCHO

b/w
dir/pro Alfred Hitchcock
st Anthony Perkins, Janet Leigh,
    Vera Miles, John Gavin

When *Psycho* was released to movie theaters in 1960, director Alfred Hitchcock insisted that no one be seated after the film had started. Audiences assumed that something terrifying would happen right at the beginning of the picture.

In fact, *Psycho* starts slowly. About halfway through the film, however, the main character, played by actress Janet Leigh, is murdered. Hitchcock said he was afraid that latecomers would miss this murder scene. Then they would be bothered for the rest of the film, wondering what had happened to their favorite star.

"We All Go a Little Mad Sometimes"
One hot Friday afternoon in Phoenix, Arizona, Marion

Crane quarrels with her boyfriend. Marion loves Sam Loomis and wants to marry him, but Sam has no money. He barely earns enough to support himself. Sam has come all the way from California to visit Marion, but now he must return home, sad and frustrated.

Marion hurries back to work, and soon an important customer enters. He senses that Marion is unhappy. "You know what I do about unhappiness?" he says. "I buy it off." With that, he takes out $40,000 and throws it on Marion's desk. The money, the customer says, is the payment for a house he is buying from Marion's boss.

Marion's boss tells her to take the money to the bank. Marion brings the money home instead. She nervously packs a suitcase. Then she sits down on the bed, trying to stop herself from doing something she knows is wrong. It is no use. Marion puts the money in her purse, picks up her suitcase, and leaves.

Driving out of Phoenix, Marion stops at a red light, and her boss sees her. He gives her a startled look. He seems to be wondering why Marion is leaving town.

The next morning, Marion wakes up in the front seat of her car. She is parked alongside the highway, hundreds of miles from Phoenix. Still sleepy, Marion suddenly sees a man with big dark glasses staring at her through the car window. To her horror, she realizes that he is a policeman.

Marion tries to act calm, but the policeman can sense that she is nervous. Marion explains to the officer that she felt drowsy while driving, so she pulled over to the side of the road. The policeman checks Marion's driver's license, then lets her go, but he is still suspicious.

Marion drives to a small town, where she trades in her car for a newer model that nobody will recognize. She pays for the new car with $700 of her stolen money.

Marion wakes up to find a policeman staring into her car.

Late that Saturday night, Marion finds herself once again falling asleep at the wheel. Lost and tired, she does not realize that she is only 15 miles from Sam's town. Up ahead, Marion sees a bright neon sign: Bates Motel.

Marion stops her car in front of the motel office and hurries inside. No one seems to be working at the motel. From the porch outside the office, Marion can see a huge, gloomy old house. Inside the house, an old woman sits beside a lighted window. Marion leans into her car and honks the horn. In a minute, Norman Bates, a friendly, thin young man, comes rushing down from the house.

Norman is delighted to have a guest staying at his

motel. "Nobody ever stops here anymore," he says. "They moved the highway." Norman picks up Marion's suitcase and leads her to cabin number one. He shows Marion where everything is. When he shows her the bathroom, however, he starts to stammer. He cannot bring himself to say the word "bathroom," as if it is a dirty word.

Marion finds Norman rather charming. He is young, awkward, and eager to please. When he invites her to the house for supper, she agrees to come. Norman tells her to wait in her room while he fetches an umbrella. While Norman is gone, Marion takes out her stolen money, folds it inside a newspaper, and places it on the nightstand.

Through the open window, Marion hears voices coming from the big house. Norman and his mother are fighting. "No, I tell you. No!" the mother screams. "I won't let you bring strange young girls in for supper."

"Shut up!" Norman yells. "Shut up!"

A few minutes later, Norman appears at Marion's door carrying a tray of sandwiches and milk. Marion invites Norman into her room, but the invitation makes him uncomfortable. Instead, he asks her to join him in the parlor behind his office. The walls of the parlor are covered with stuffed birds, hawks and crows and owls with their wings spread wide. "My hobby is stuffing things," Norman says.

Marion tries to get Norman to talk about himself, but he is shy. "Do you go out with friends?" Marion asks. "Well," Norman says, "a boy's best friend is his mother."

Norman explains that his mother is mentally ill and he has to take care of her, even though she treats him badly. When Marion suggests that Norman put his mother in an institution, he becomes angry and defensive. "We all go a little mad sometimes," he says. "Haven't you?"

Marion checks in for a fateful evening at the Bates Motel.

Norman Bates hurries to put Marion's dead body into his car's trunk.

"Yes," says Marion. "Sometimes just one time can be enough." As Marion talks with Norman, she realizes how horrible life can be when you are trapped in a situation you cannot escape. By stealing her boss's money, she has placed herself in just such a trap. "I have a long drive tomorrow," she tells Norman, "all the way back to Phoenix. I stepped into a private trap back there, and I'd like to go back and try to pull myself out of it."

That night in her room, Marion plans to return the stolen money. On a scrap of paper, she figures out a way to repay the $700 she spent on her new car. Then she tears up the paper and flushes it down the toilet.

Marion gets undressed and climbs into the shower. She is tired but happy, because she knows she is going to do the right thing. Marion never sees the bathroom door open and a shadow sneaking up to the shower.

Suddenly, the shower curtain is pulled back. Marion screams helplessly as a huge knife blade stabs her over and over and over. In just a few seconds, Marion is lying dead in the tub, her eyes wide open, her blood trickling down the drain.

Back at the house, Norman Bates screams in anguish. "Mother, oh Mother," he cries. "Blood, blood." Within minutes Norman is inside Marion's room carrying a mop and pail. He wraps Marion's body in the shower curtain, then scrubs the bathroom clean. He loads Marion's body and her belongings into the trunk of her car. The last thing he finds in the room is Marion's rolled-up newspaper. Without looking inside it, he tosses the paper into the car trunk and slams the lid shut.

Norman drives Marion's car to a swamp behind the motel. He gets out and pushes the car into a deep pool. The black waters of the swamp cover the car completely.

A week later, on a dark, cloudy night, a private detective named Arbogast arrives at the Bates Motel. He has been hired by Marion's boss to recover the stolen $40,000.

Norman Bates does not like Arbogast. The slickly dressed, fast-talking man makes Norman uneasy. Arbogast traps Norman in lie after lie. When Norman says that Marion never stopped at the motel, Arbogast proves she did by finding a sample of her handwriting in the motel register. Finally, Arbogast asks to talk to Norman's mother. Norman tells the private detective to go away.

Arbogast does go away, but not far. At a phone booth, he calls Sam Loomis. Sam is waiting at the hardware store with Marion's sister Lila. Lila has flown to California to search for Marion. Arbogast tells Sam and Lila that Norman Bates knows more than he is telling. He says he will report back to them just as soon as he talks to Norman's mother.

Arbogast then returns to the old, dark house. He sneaks inside and quietly walks upstairs. At the top of the stairs, Arbogast calls softly for Mrs. Bates.

All at once a door flies open and an old woman rushes across the landing, a knife held high. She cuts Arbogast across the forehead. Losing his balance, the detective tumbles backwards down the stairs. When he comes to a stop, the old woman is on top of him in an instant, stabbing him with the knife.

Later, when Arbogast fails to return, Sam and Lila go to the sheriff. The sheriff suspects that Arbogast himself may have found the missing money and disappeared. It is unlikely that the detective went back to talk to Norman's mother. "Norman Bates's mother has been dead and buried for the past 10 years," the sheriff says. Mrs. Bates poisoned herself after first killing her boyfriend.

Sam and Lila decide to investigate the Bates Motel themselves.

Sam and Lila refuse to believe that Arbogast ran out on them. The next day they drive to the Bates Motel and register as guests. Norman shows them to their room. At first he opens the door to cabin number one, then he changes his mind and takes them to another cabin. Sam and Lila notice this. A half hour later, they are searching cabin number one. Lila finds a scrap of paper inside the toilet bowl. The paper says "$40,000."

Convinced that Marion stayed at the Bates Motel, they form a plan. Sam will talk to Norman while Lila sneaks up to the house. The plan works well until Norman realizes what is happening. Then he slugs Sam with a vase and rushes up to the house.

Meanwhile, inside the house, Lila finds rooms full of furniture and old clothes, but no sign of Mrs. Bates. When she hears Norman running up the front steps, Lila hides in the fruit cellar. There she is surprised to find Mrs. Bates, sitting in a chair, her back to Lila. Lila calls softly to the old woman, then walks over and taps her on the shoulder.

The chair spins around. The old woman's face is a horrible, dried-up death mask with gaping holes where the eyes should be. As Lila screams in terror, Norman rushes into the cellar, his knife held high. He is wearing a woman's dress and wig—the same dress and wig he wore when he killed Marion and Arbogast. Just as Norman starts to stab Lila, Sam runs down the stairs and grabs him from behind. Sam wrestles the insane man to the ground.

That afternoon, a police psychiatrist explains to Sam and Lila the strange, twisted life of Norman Bates. As a boy, Norman was jealous of his mother's boyfriend, so he poisoned both his mother and her boyfriend. That horrible deed upset Norman so much that he tried to erase its memory. He kept his mother's body inside the house, stuffed like one of his birds. But even that was not enough to keep his mother alive in Norman's mind. "He began to think and speak for her," the psychiatrist says.

"Did he kill my sister?" Lila asks.

"Yes," the psychiatrist says, "and no." Norman let the mother-side of his personality control him. When he tried to make friends with other women, his jealous "mother" would take over. It was Norman, acting as his mother, who killed Marion.

In another room of the police station, Norman sits huddled beneath a blanket. His eyes stare off into space, but inside his head, his mother's voice is talking. "They're probably watching me," Norman says in his high-pitched

One of the world's most famous movie directors, Alfred Hitchcock made dozens of films. Critics and audiences alike love his movies, which include *Rear Window, Vertigo, The Man Who Knew Too Much,* and *Notorious.*

mother's voice. "Let them." He looks down at a fly crawling on his hand, but he does not move a muscle. He just grins. "Let them see what kind of a person I am," he says. "They'll say, 'Why, she wouldn't even hurt a fly.' "

THE FAMOUS SHOWER SCENE

The scene in *Psycho* in which Marion is killed in the shower is one of the most famous scenes in the history of motion pictures. Although the scene lasts only 45 seconds on-screen, it took 7 days to film. The camera was repositioned 70 times to record long shots, close shots, and many different angles.

At one point, the film crew tried substituting a dummy for actress Janet Leigh, but the resulting film did not look real. Director Alfred Hitchcock did not think it was proper for a star like Janet Leigh to be seen without her clothes. So he used a fashion model as a stand-in for the star. In the final version of the shower scene, only Janet Leigh's hands, shoulders, and head appear. The body that seems to get stabbed belongs to the stand-in.

Hitchcock originally planned to use only the sounds of running water and Marion's screams in the shower scene. Music composer Bernard Herrmann, however, asked the director to listen to some music he had written for the scene. Herrmann's music featured screeching violins that sounded like angry birds. This music not only added to the violence of the scene, it also subtly reminded viewers of Norman Bates's interest in birds. After listening to Herrmann's music, Hitchcock had to admit that it improved the scene.

After *Psycho* was finished, Hitchcock showed the film to his wife, Alma. She spotted a problem with the shower scene that no one else had noticed. "Hitch," she said, "Janet Leigh gulps after she is supposed to be dead." The director realized that his wife was right. He had to return to the editing room and snip out one second of film in order to make Janet Leigh look really dead.

THE EXORCIST

color
dir William Friedkin
pro William Peter Blatty
st Ellen Burstyn, Max von Sydow,
   Lee J. Cobb, Linda Blair
makeup Dick Smith

The *Exorcist* opened at theaters in New York City in December 1973. Before long, local newspapers were reporting that dozens of viewers had fainted, vomited, or been carried from theaters on stretchers. In response to these stories, the film's director, William Friedkin, said, "When people get carried out on stretchers in my movie, I say they get what they paid for. They went in to be shocked and scared."

The film's effect on audiences was partly due to its story. Many Americans grew up hearing about the power of the devil. Watching *The Exorcist*, viewers remembered the frightening stories they had heard in church or religion classes when they were children.

"The Child Is Mine"

Deep in the desert of Iraq, archaeologists discover a temple that is thousands of years old and seems to have been built by people who worshipped the devil.

Father Lancaster Merrin, a Catholic priest and archaeologist, walks through the temple ruins. He clutches at his chest, as if his heart causes him pain. All around him, Merrin feels the presence of the devil. The devil seems to be challenging him to fight. Although he is old and tired, Father Merrin is not afraid. He has met the devil before.

Thousands of miles away, in Washington, D.C., a movie actress named Chris MacNeil is having trouble sleeping. A noise in the attic keeps waking her up. Chris rolls over and is surprised to find her 12-year-old daughter Regan lying in bed next to her. Regan can't sleep either. "My bed was shaking," she says. Chris and Regan do not know it yet, but something evil has entered their house.

Across town, the MacNeils' neighbor, Father Damien Karras, waits for a train to New York City. Karras is going to visit his mother, a sick old woman who lives by herself. Lying on the floor of the train station, a tattered old beggar calls to Karras. "Father," he says, "could you help an old altar boy?" Father Karras, wrapped up in his own problems, turns his back on the man.

A few nights later, Chris MacNeil throws a big party at her house. Chris asks one of her friends, Father Dyer, about her neighbor, the handsome young priest. "That's Damien Karras," Father Dyer says. He tells Chris that Karras has just suffered a terrible loss. His mother died, alone in a hospital, calling for her son.

Toward the end of the party, Regan comes downstairs in her nightgown. She acts as if she is in a trance. She turns to one of the party guests, an astronaut who soon

Chris comforts her daughter Regan after the girl causes an embarrassing scene at Chris's party.

will be launched into space. "You're going to die up there," Regan says. Then she urinates on the floor.

Embarrassed and confused, Chris helps her daughter upstairs and gives her a hot bath. "Mother," Regan says, "what's wrong with me?" Chris tells Regan that she is upset because of all the changes she has experienced in the last few months. First, Regan's father left them, then Chris's job brought them to a new town. Chris puts Regan to bed and promises her that everything will be all right.

As soon as she leaves the bedroom, however, Chris hears Regan screaming. Rushing back into the room, Chris sees something she cannot believe. Regan's bed is bucking wildly, bouncing up and down on the floor. Chris throws herself on top of Regan until the bed stops bouncing.

The next day, Chris takes Regan to see a doctor. The doctor tells Chris that Regan probably has suffered an injury to her brain. That would explain her strange behavior. He says the bucking bed was the result of muscle spasms, powerful and uncontrollable body movements. "Mrs. MacNeil," the doctor says, "the problem with your daughter is not her bed, it's her brain."

A team of doctors performs a series of painful tests on Regan. To their surprise, they find nothing wrong with her. A few nights later, Chris MacNeil asks the doctors to come to her house. When they arrive, Chris leads them upstairs to Regan's bedroom.

Regan is jerking back and forth on the bed, her body whipping backwards and forwards. Then she bounces into the air. "Make it stop!" Regan screams. "He's trying to kill me."

When one of the doctors reaches for Regan, she slaps him across the face, knocking him to the floor. Then a strange, deep voice comes out of Regan's mouth. "Keep away," the voice says. "The child is mine."

Over the next few days, more tests—all of them terribly painful—reveal nothing wrong with Regan's brain. The girl is pale and exhausted, with dark rings around her eyes.

One night, after talking with another doctor, Chris comes home and finds Regan lying on her bed in a freezing cold room. Chris is furious. A friend was supposed to be watching Regan while Chris was out. How could he have left her alone like this?

The doorbell rings. Standing on the front porch is a young man who works with Chris. "I guess you haven't heard," he says. A half hour earlier, Chris's friend was found dead at the bottom of a long flight of stairs outside Regan's bedroom window.

On a cold autumn day, Chris MacNeil stands alone on a footbridge, waiting to meet Father Damien Karras. Chris thinks Father Karras may be her last hope. She believes a religious ritual might save her daughter. The ritual, called an exorcism, is the way that Catholic priests drive the devil out of people.

When Father Karras meets Chris, he tries to tell her that he does not believe in exorcisms. "I've never met one priest who has performed an exorcism. Not one."

Chris begs Father Karras to talk to Regan, and he reluctantly agrees. When he enters Regan's bedroom, he sees a small, helpless girl strapped to a padded bed. Her face is cut, her hair is matted, and her eyes look wild. When Father Karras asks Regan who she is, a deep voice responds, "I'm the devil."

"Where's Regan?" Father Karras asks.

"In here," growls the voice, "with us."

Then the voice takes on a soft, pleading tone, one that Karras has heard before. "Can you help an old altar boy, Father?" the voice says. Karras leans closer, shocked. At that moment, Regan spits thick green slime all over him.

Later, Father Karras tells Chris that the Catholic Church insists on proof that the devil really is inside a person. One sign is for a person to speak in a language she does not know, so Karras returns to Regan's bedroom with a tape recorder.

Karras records many strange voices that seem to be coming from inside Regan. He takes the tape to a sound expert, who says it's English in reverse. The expert plays the tape backwards for Father Karras. A deep voice curses and calls out the name "Merrin" over and over.

The next time Father Karras visits the MacNeil house, Chris's secretary takes him into Regan's bedroom. "I don't

Father Merrin hopes to drive the devil out of Regan.

want Chris to see this," the secretary says. She lifts up the nightgown of the sleeping Regan. The skin on Regan's stomach rises up, forming the words "HELP ME."

Father Karras is convinced that an exorcism must be performed. He visits his bishop, who sends for Lancaster Merrin. "He's had experience," the bishop says.

Father Merrin arrives on a dark, foggy night. He looks up at Regan's window. His old enemy seems to be calling him. As he enters the house, he hears a horrible voice screaming from Regan's bedroom. "Merrin!" it cries.

Father Karras tells Father Merrin that Regan has three different personalities, three voices inside her. Merrin interrupts him. "There is only one," he says. He warns Father

Karras not to listen to the devil's voice. "He is a liar," Father Merrin says. "But he will mix lies with the truth."

Inside Regan's bedroom, the air is icy cold, as if the devil had sucked all warmth out of the room. The devil's voice curses Father Merrin. Merrin splashes Regan's body with holy water and yells, "Be silent!" Regan screams and twists away, as if the holy water burns her.

Father Merrin recites the Lord's Prayer, then reads the lines of the exorcism ritual. As Merrin and Karras pray desperately, Regan slowly rises off her bed and floats in midair. Father Karras is astounded, but Father Merrin prays even harder. Regan slowly sinks back onto her bed.

The devil has not given up, however. He makes Regan sit up in bed and spit green slime on the priests. Then her head turns 360 degrees. A horrible, purple tongue darts in and out of her mouth. The room's walls and ceiling crack, and lamps crash to the floor. Worst of all for Father Karras, when he looks at Regan, he sees his own dead mother calling to him.

The two priests stagger out of the bedroom. They need to rest. Father Merrin takes medicine for his weak heart, then goes back into the bedroom. A few minutes later, Father Karras joins him, but it is too late. The old priest is dead. Regan is sitting by a bedpost, smiling.

Father Karras jumps on Regan, tossing her to the floor. He hits her with his fist. "Come into me," Karras shouts at the devil inside Regan. "Come into me."

Suddenly Karras's eyes roll back in his head. His face takes on a terrible appearance. His arms and legs move as if someone else is controlling them. The devil has entered his body. With all his might, Karras stands, struggling against the devil. He screams horribly, then throws himself out of the bedroom window.

The devil — and lots of makeup — have transformed an innocent little girl into a fiendish monster.

Father Karras lands outside, at the bottom of a steep flight of stairs. Just before Karras dies, Father Dyer tells him that God has forgiven him for his sins.

A few weeks later, Chris and Regan pack up to return to their home in Los Angeles. Regan is healthy and happy. Chris turns to Father Dyer. "She doesn't remember any of it," Chris says. But when Regan sees Father Dyer's priest's collar, she kisses the priest on the cheek, as if to say "Thank you."

COLD ROOMS AND LIQUID RUBBER

Although some viewers appreciated *The Exorcist*'s religious story, others simply responded to the film's startling special effects. To turn the young actress Linda Blair into Regan, the devil's victim, makeup artist Dick Smith employed many clever tricks. Regan's frightening, "devilish" eyes were created with yellow contact lenses. Her ripped flesh was made from liquid rubber, and her rotating head was really a dummy with radio-controlled eyes. The green slime Regan spit on Father Karras and Father Merrin was a mixture of oatmeal and pea soup.

Many of the film's scenes were shot on location in Iraq and Washington, D.C. Regan's bedroom, however, was a special refrigerated set built on a soundstage in New York City. This cold set caused the actors' breath to steam up in the icy presence of the devil. Altogether, $12 million was spent to make *The Exorcist* one of the most powerful and successful horror films of all time.

Freddy is not your average nightmare — he's for real.

A NIGHTMARE ON ELM STREET

color
dir Wes Craven
pro Robert Shaye
st Amanda Wyss, Heather
   Langenkamp, Ronee Blakely,
   Robert Englund

When director Wes Craven first showed *A Nightmare on Elm Street* to the heads of the big Hollywood movie studios, no one wanted to buy it. They told Craven that movies about dreams were not popular. So Craven found a small company to distribute his film to movie theaters. The film was an immediate hit, particularly with young audiences. With its four sequels, *A Nightmare on Elm Street* has become one of the most popular horror film series in history.

"Whatever You Do—Don't Fall Asleep"

   Tina, a frightened teenager, is running for her life. Something—or someone—is chasing her down the dark hallways of an underground boiler room.

Tina's bare feet splash in pools of oily water. Her nightgown brushes against hot, dripping pipes. As she rounds a corner, flames from a furnace roar up in front of her. The loud, screeching sound of a knife being scraped against a pipe cuts through the air. A madman named Freddy is looking for Tina. Wherever she goes, Freddy's horrible, laughing voice comes after her.

Suddenly Freddy pops up behind Tina. She does not see him as he comes closer and closer. He wears an old hat pulled low over his face. His face has been so badly burned that he barely looks human.

Fastened to the fingers of Freddy's right hand are four long, sharp knives. Freddy lifts his knives in the air and, with a terrible laugh, grabs Tina from behind.

Just at that moment, Tina wakes up. It was only a dream, she thinks—or was it? The girl looks down at her nightgown, which has been slashed in four places, as if by knives.

The next evening, Tina asks her friend Nancy Thompson to stay with her. Nancy tells Tina that she, too, has had the same frightening dreams. "Maybe we're going to have a big earthquake," Tina says. "They say things get really weird before one."

Two boys from their high school, Rod and Glen, drop by to visit the girls. When they are alone, Rod confesses to Tina that he, too, has dreamt about the man with the "finger-knives."

Rod falls asleep, but Tina hears a voice like the wind whispering her name: "Ti-na." She walks into the back yard, not realizing that she has also fallen asleep, and the deadly dream has begun again.

In the back alley, Tina sees Freddy's shadow. His finger-knives are waving in the air. Tina turns to run away from him, but he pops up right in front of her. His arms reach out for her, stretching until they are nearly eight feet long. As Freddy grabs Tina, she scratches his face, but the skin on his face comes right off.

Suddenly, Tina and Freddy are inside the house. Tina struggles, but Freddy cuts her with his knives, then drags her right up the wall and across the ceiling.

Rod wakes up and sees Tina rolling on the ceiling. She is bleeding, as if someone is slashing her over and over again. Rod cannot see who is killing Tina, though. When she finally falls to the floor, dead, Rod is confused and terrified. Certain that the police will think he killed Tina, Rod jumps out a window and runs away.

The next day, the police arrest Rod and charge him with Tina's murder. Nancy Thompson is upset about her friend's death, but she thinks that Rod may be innocent. Since Nancy's father is a police lieutenant, she hopes he will be able to help Rod. She tells her father about Tina's horrible nightmares. Her father, however, is convinced that Rod is the killer.

Nancy's mother and father are separated, and Nancy lives with her mother, an unhappy woman who cannot handle her own problems. Nancy, on the other hand, always faces up to things. She never backs down, even when she is scared.

At school the next day, Nancy falls asleep in English class. Looking up, she sees Tina, dead and bloody, walking slowly out of the classroom. Nancy follows her.

In the corridor, Nancy pushes past a hall monitor and runs after Tina. The hall monitor calls after her. When Nancy looks back at her, the girl's fingers have turned into knives like Freddy's. Now the nightmare has begun for Nancy.

In her dream, Nancy follows Tina into a basement boiler room. Tina disappears, but the man with the burned face jumps out from behind a dripping pipe. "Come to Freddy," he says. Nancy knows she cannot escape, so she presses her arm against a hot pipe, hoping the pain will wake her up. "It's only a dream," she screams.

Nancy does wake up. She is sitting at her desk in English class, screaming. Looking down, Nancy sees a burn on her arm—the burn from the hot pipe in her dream. Now Nancy understands that her dreams are real. If Freddy catches her, she's dead.

Nancy begins to do everything she can to stay awake. She drinks coffee and listens to loud music at night. She even watches horror movies on television. But one night she falls asleep in the bathtub. Freddy's hand rises out of the water and pulls her down into a bathtub that seems to be as deep as a well. Nancy is saved when her mother's worried cries wake her up, making Freddy disappear.

That same night, Freddy visits Rod in his jail cell. As Rod sleeps on his cot, Freddy makes the sheet come alive. The sheet twists around Rod's neck, then strangles him.

At Rod's funeral, Nancy tells her father, "The killer's still loose, you know." Nancy's father just shakes his head sadly. He thinks that his daughter is being driven crazy by the death of her friends.

Nancy's mother takes Nancy to a hospital. There doctors use a special machine to record the brain waves of sleeping people. As Nancy slips into a deep sleep, the machine's needles move smoothly up and down. They show that Nancy is having a normal, relaxing dream. Dreams are an important part of life, one of the doctors tells Nancy's mother. "If you don't dream, you go crazy."

Just then, the needles on the brain-wave machine begin

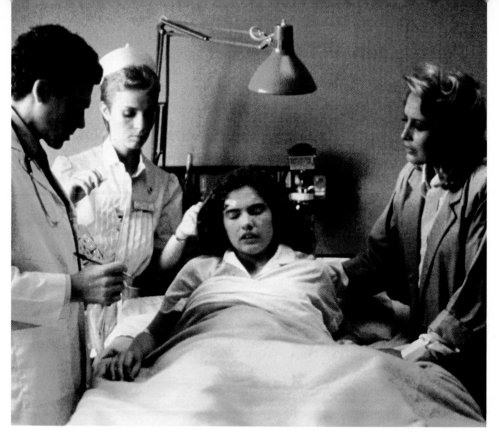

Nancy's mother takes her to a hospital, where doctors monitor her sleep to see what might be causing her strange "dreams."

to bounce wildly. Nancy jerks and screams. Her mother and one of the doctors rush into her room to wake her up. As Nancy sits up in bed, sobbing, she feels something under the covers. She reaches down and pulls out Freddy's dirty, battered hat. "I brought something out from my dream," she says.

At home the next day, Nancy finds a name written inside the hat: "Fred Kruger." Nancy's mother tells her that Fred Kruger was a murderer who killed 20 children. When the police did not put Kruger in jail, Nancy's mother joined a group of parents that tracked him down. The parents found Kruger in an old boiler room and set him on fire. "He's dead, honey," Nancy's mother says, "because Mommy killed him." She shows Nancy a small sack she has kept hidden in the cellar. "I even took his knives," Nancy's mother says, pulling Freddy's finger-knives out of the sack.

What Nancy's mother does not understand is that Freddy is still alive in the dreams of the children who live on Elm Street. "It's just a nightmare," Nancy's mother says. "That's enough," Nancy replies.

Nancy forces herself to stay awake for six nights in a row. Her skin turns pale, dark circles form under her eyes, and her hair begins to turn gray. "I look like I'm 20 years old," Nancy says sadly.

At the library, Nancy finds books on booby traps. Nancy's friend Glen tells her about people on the island of Bali who developed a special system of "dream-skills." "For instance, if they fall in their dreams," Glen says, "they fall into a magic world of a poem or a song."

"Well, what if they meet a monster in their dreams," Nancy says. "Then what?"

"They turn their back on it," Glen says. "Take away its energy and it disappears."

Nancy still thinks her booby traps are the best defense against Freddy. She persuades Glen to help her capture the madman. First, Nancy will fall asleep and find Freddy. Then, when her alarm clock goes off, she will grab Freddy and bring him out of her dream with her. At that point, she wants Glen to be waiting with a baseball bat.

The teenagers agree to meet at midnight. "Whatever you do," Nancy says, "don't fall asleep."

At midnight, Nancy goes to the window. Glen's house is just across Elm Street. Nancy can see Glen upstairs in his bedroom, sound asleep. She phones Glen, but his father refuses to let her talk to him. Furious, Nancy rips her phone out of the wall. She starts to leave her room, but the phone rings. Nancy moves toward it slowly, looking at the disconnected cord. She picks up the receiver and hears the voice she fears most. "I'm your boyfriend now, Nancy," Freddy says. A purple tongue darts out of the mouthpiece of the phone, and Nancy drops it in fear and disgust.

Nancy runs downstairs to warn Glen, but she cannot get out of her own house. Her mother has locked the doors and put bars on all the windows. Across the street, Freddy reaches up through a hole in Glen's bed and pulls the boy down to a bloody death.

As police cars arrive outside Glen's house, Nancy makes up her mind what she is going to do. She begins to plant booby traps around her house: exploding light bulbs, trip wires, falling sledge hammers. Then she sets her alarm clock and lies down to sleep. "O.K., Kruger," she says. "We play in your court."

Soon Nancy is dreaming, searching the boiler room, looking for Freddy. She checks her wristwatch. It is almost time for her alarm to go off. Nancy looks up and sees Freddy leaping towards her, his finger-knives flashing. Nancy jumps out of the way, then grabs Freddy as the alarm clock begins to ring. She wakes up in her bedroom, alone. Freddy is nowhere in sight.

Nancy sits on her bed, feeling sad and confused. "I'm crazy after all," she says. Then, from beneath the bed, she hears the horrible, mad laughter of Freddy Kruger. Nancy *has* brought Freddy back from her dream. He leaps up from the floor, but Nancy dodges him and runs downstairs. She calls to the policeman across the street. "Get my dad," she yells.

"I'm your boyfriend now, Nancy," Freddy tells the horrified girl.

Freddy comes bursting out of Nancy's bedroom, only to get hit in the stomach by a falling sledge hammer. Then a hidden trip wire sends him tumbling down the stairs. At the foot of the stairs, Nancy douses Freddy with gasoline and sets him on fire.

Nancy's father breaks down the front door, and she takes him to see Freddy's body. Instead of a body, however, they see fiery footprints leading to Nancy's mother's bedroom.

Rushing upstairs, Nancy and her father find a pool of flashing light in the middle of Nancy's mother's bed.

Nancy's mother and Freddy are both gone. Nancy's father is shaken and confused, but Nancy knows what she must do. "You go downstairs," she says to her father. "I'll be there in a minute."

When her father is gone, the bedroom door closes by itself. The bed comes alive as Freddy begins to slash through the sheets. He is coming for Nancy one last time. She turns her back on him. "I know you too well now, Freddy," she says. "I know the secret now. This whole thing is just a dream. I want my mother and friends again. I take back every bit of energy I gave you. You're nothing."

Freddy lunges toward Nancy's back, but he dissolves in a pool of light before he gets there. Nancy opens the bedroom door and steps outside. She finds herself on the front porch, standing in bright sunlight. She is smiling, and her hair is no longer gray.

A car pulls up in front of the house, and Glen and Rod and Tina wave to Nancy. As Nancy runs to join them, she turns and sees her mother standing on the front porch, waving at the kids. The nightmare is over.

But as Glen starts to drive away, his car goes crazy. The doors lock themselves, and the windows roll themselves up. Nancy screams a warning to her mother, but it is too late. Freddy's arm comes through the door, wraps around Mrs. Thompson, and pulls her inside. The nightmare on Elm Street is not over yet.

A SURPRISE HIT AND A SURPRISE STAR

Wes Craven says young people like the *Nightmare* films because they show the importance of facing up to evil. Too many adults have learned to live with the fear of crime, war, and even nuclear destruction. "You know," says

Director Wes Craven and Amanda Wyss, who plays Nancy's mother, consult on the set of *A Nightmare on Elm Street.* The set has been built "upside-down" to film the scene on the ceiling.

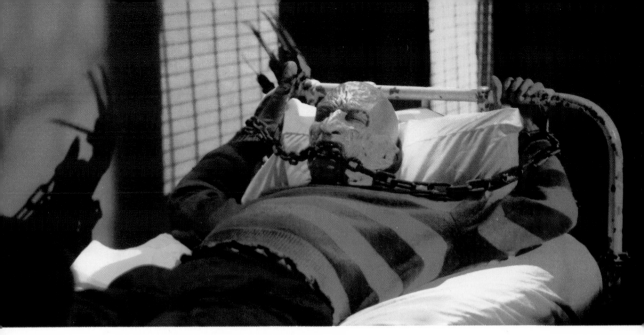

Freddy lives on in the TV series "Freddy's Nightmares."

Craven, "there's a million ways that we in our culture sleep and try to check out of what's really going on. Nancy stayed awake, she took responsibility for being a conscious human being, and it's the one thing that saved her life while everyone else slept and died."

Like the film itself, the villain of *A Nightmare on Elm Street*, Freddy Kruger, has become surprisingly popular. Besides appearing in three more *Nightmare* movies, Freddy has starred in his own TV series, "Freddy's Nightmares." He has been featured in posters and rap songs and appeared as a guest "veejay" on the music video stations.

Yet Freddy is still a scary figure, a child murderer. Actor Robert Englund, who plays Freddy, says, "I think that what Freddy *really* stands for is the idea of killing the future: he has no place there, and so he is killing it. He has an envy of youth, and when teenagers see these movies, I'm sure that's what really freaks them out and scares them."

For Further Reading

Aylesworth, Thomas G. *Monsters from the Movies.* Philadelphia: J.B. Lippincott Company, 1972.

Cohen, Daniel. *Horror in the Movies.* New York: Clarion Books, 1982.

————. *Horror Movies.* New York: Gallery Books, 1984.

————. *Masters of Horror.* New York: Clarion Books, 1984.

Edelson, Edward. *Great Monsters of the Movies.* Garden City, N.Y.: Doubleday & Company, 1973.

Everson, William K. *More Classics of the Horror Film.* Secaucus, N.J.: Citadel Press, 1986.

Manchel, Frank. *Terrors of the Screen.* Englewood Cliffs, N.J.: Prentice-Hall, 1970.

Index